Reading Essentials®
in Science

HUMAN LIVING SYSTEMS

Cell
Processes

KAREN BLEDSOE

PERFECTION LEARNING®

Editorial Director: Susan C. Thies
Editor: Mary L. Bush
Design Director: Randy Messer
Book Design: Tobi S. Cunningham
Cover Design: Michael A. Aspengren

A special thanks to the following for his scientific review of the book:
Paul Pistek, Instructor of Biological Sciences,
North Iowa Area Community College

Image credits:
©Jim Zuckerman/CORBIS: p. 6; ©CDC/PHIL/CORBIS: p. 7; ©Visuals Unlimited/CORBIS:
p. 8 (top left); ©Visuals Unlimited/Corbis: p. 10; ©Carol and Mike Werner/Phototake:
p. 19 (top); ©Howard Sochurek/CORBIS: p. 24 (top); ©ISM/Phototake: p. 25; ©Dennis
Kunkel/Phototake: p. 29; ©Eurelios/Phototake: p. 32

Photos.com: front and back cover, pp. 2–3, 16–17 (bottom), 18–19 (bottom), 21 (bottom),
22–23 (bottom), 26–27 (bottom), 30, 30–31 (bottom), 31, 32–33 (bottom), 33, 34, 35, 36;
Istock.com: pp. 1, 4–5 (bottom), 8 (top middle), 8 (top right), 8 (bottom), 9, 12, 15, 28;
Clipart.com: all side backgrounds, p. 5 (top); Perfection Learning Corporation: pp. 11, 13,
14, 17 (top), 23, 24 (bottom), 26

For information, contact
Perfection Learning® Corporation
1000 North Second Avenue, P.O. Box 500
Logan, Iowa 51546-0500.
Phone: 1-800-831-4190
Fax: 1-800-543-2745
perfectionlearning.com

1 2 3 4 5 6 PP 11 10 09 08 07 06
PB ISBN 0-7891-6985-1
RLB ISBN 0-7569-6385-0

Table of Contents

1. Cells—You Can't Live Without 'Em 4

2. A Protein Factory 10

3. From Food to Energy 18

4. The Cell Cycle 22

5. Cellular Current Events 28

Internet Connections and
Related Reading for Cell Processes 37

Glossary 38

Index 40

chapter one

Cells—

You Can't Live Without 'Em

Every living thing on Earth, from bacteria to blue whales, is made of cells. Cells are the smallest units of life. Some organisms, such as bacteria, are made of only one cell. Others, such as humans, are multicellular, or made of many cells. Whether an organism has one cell or one billion cells, its existence is dependent on these amazing tiny pieces of life.

Cell Beginnings

Two men were important to the discovery of cells in the mid-1600s. Robert Hooke used early microscopes to spot tiny box-shaped structures in pieces of cork from an oak tree. He called the structures *cells* because they reminded him of the rooms in a monastery where monks slept.

Anton van Leeuwenhoek

Anton van Leeuwenhoek built microscopes and used them to study the tiny organisms found in the world around him. He called these organisms *animalcules*. Animalcules later became known as organisms such as bacteria, protozoans, and molds. The discoveries made by these two men opened a whole new world to be studied.

Inside the Cell

Because cells are so small, it took almost 200 years to learn more about their composition. Finally, in the 1800s, the invention of better light microscopes allowed scientists to look inside tiny cells. In 1831, Robert Brown, an English botanist, identified a structure in the middle of plant cells. He called this structure a **nucleus**. In 1839, Matthias Schleiden and Theodor Schwann combined their work on plant and animal cells and proposed the cell theory. This theory stated that all living things are made of cells. In the mid-1850s, Rudolph Virchow added to the theory with the idea that all cells come from other cells.

In the 1930s, the electron microscope made it possible to dig even deeper into the cell and led to the discovery of many cell structures. Over time, scientists were able to develop modern theories and models of the human cell.

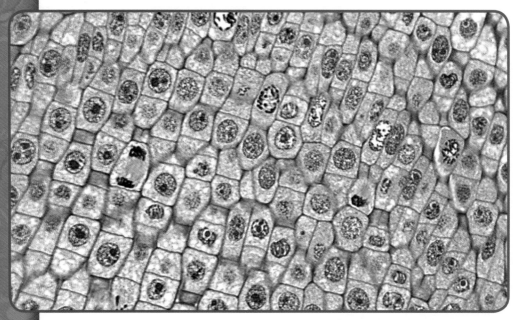

Human skin cells

A microbiologist scans bacteria cells with a scanning electron microscope.

Technology Link

Light microscopes use glass lenses to focus light and magnify an object. But no matter how strong the lens is, a light microscope is limited by its resolution (ability to produce a sharp image with fine details). Resolution is determined by the wavelengths of light that enter a microscope. Modern light microscopes can achieve a magnification of up to 5000 times by using blue light. This may sound like a lot, but it's nothing compared to the electron microscope.

In 1931, physicist Ernst Ruska used magnets to focus a beam of electrons onto an object. An image of the object was then projected onto a screen. The images from Ruska's microscope showed much more detail than light microscopes had previously revealed. Ruska's microscope became known as the electron microscope. The best electron microscopes today can magnify objects up to 2 million times!

Cell Facts

Today it is known that all life on Earth is composed of the living, growing bodies called *cells*. These bodies come in a variety of shapes and sizes. Cell shapes are as varied as their functions. Cells are shaped like boxes, rods, disks, spirals, or irregular blobs. Animals, including humans, have the greatest variety in the shapes of their cells.

White blood cells

Red blood cells

Human egg cell

Most cells are so small that they can't be seen without a microscope. However, they still vary in size from one another. The largest human cell, the egg, is about one-tenth of a millimeter in diameter, making it barely visible to the naked eye. Skin cells, white blood cells, and many other human cells are about one-tenth the size of an egg—only one-hundredth of a millimeter or smaller in diameter. The nerve cells that run from the big toe to the spine can be more than a meter long, but they're extremely thin (about one-tenth of the diameter of a human hair or less).

Larger organisms aren't made of bigger cells than smaller organisms. Larger organisms just have *more* cells than smaller ones. Humans, for example, don't have larger cells than rabbits, but they have more cells than rabbits.

The human body is made up of trillions of cells. Not all of these cells are the same though. There are actually about 220 different kinds of cells that work together in the human body. Each type of cell in a body specializes in a specific job. Nerve cells carry messages. Skin cells form a wall of protection. White blood cells battle germs. Together, all of the cells in a body make up one successful living team.

chapter two

A Protein Factory

A cell is a busy place where all the processes of human life occur. It is similar to a factory. A factory needs a building and raw materials. It also needs a power source and workers to run the machinery. A cell needs materials and a source of energy too. It has structures, or organelles, that perform jobs in the cell. Ultimately, each cell's "finished product" contributes to the health and functioning of the body.

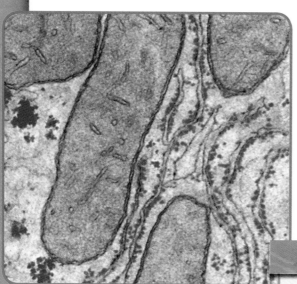

Organelles in a liver cell

Organelles

The word *organelle* means "little organ." Organs are body parts. Organelles are little parts of cells.

One of the important jobs of cells is to manufacture **proteins**. Proteins are a group of molecules that makes up all cells and directs their activities. It is estimated that humans have about one million different proteins.

Cells in the human pancreas make a protein called *insulin*. Insulin is needed to move sugar from the blood into cells. Let's look at the process of making insulin to see how a cell factory works.

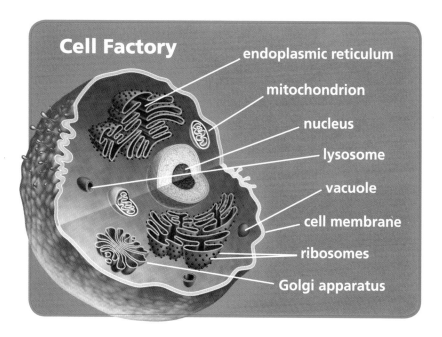

Cell Factory

endoplasmic reticulum
mitochondrion
nucleus
lysosome
vacuole
cell membrane
ribosomes
Golgi apparatus

The Building Walls

Like a factory needs a building, all cells have a **cell membrane** to separate the inside of the cell from its outer environment. The cell membrane is a thin, flexible layer of fat and protein. The membrane acts like a security guard. It allows certain substances in and out, while keeping other substances from entering or leaving the cell.

To create insulin, a pancreas cell needs **amino acids**. Amino acids are the building blocks of proteins. A cell's membrane transports amino acids from the bloodstream into the cell.

The Boss's Office and the Instruction Manual

The boss of the cell, the nucleus, is located within its own membrane. Like the boss of a factory, the nucleus controls all of the cell's activities. It sends messages to the other "workers," or parts of the cell, telling them what to do.

Named for a Nucleus

Because human cells have a nucleus, they are called *eukaryotic cells*. Eukaryotic cells also have organelles that are enclosed in a membrane. All plant and animal cells are eukaryotic. Other cells, such as bacteria, do not have a nucleus or organelles with membranes. These cells are called *prokaryotic cells*.

To put the amino acids together in the correct order, a pancreas cell needs a set of instructions. These instructions are contained in **DNA** (deoxyribonucleic acid), which is found in the cell's nucleus. DNA makes up a person's **genes**. A gene is the instruction for a characteristic of a cell.

A model of DNA

When a pancreas cell needs to make insulin, it makes a copy of the gene for insulin. The copy is made of a material similar to DNA called *mRNA* (messenger ribonucleic acid). The original DNA stays in the nucleus, while the mRNA carries the instructions to the protein-making parts of the cell.

What's Inside a Cell?

All of the living material inside a cell, except for the nucleus, is called the *cytoplasm*. Most of the cytoplasm is a jellylike substance made of water and dissolved nutrients. A cell's organelles "swim" in this watery gel.

The Protein Assembly Line

The mRNA molecules are released into the cytoplasm, where they come in contact with **ribosomes**. Ribosomes read the codes on the mRNA and look for matching codes on other RNA molecules called *tRNA* (transfer ribonucleic acid). These tRNA molecules carry amino acids. When codes on mRNA and tRNA match, the ribosomes use the amino acids to make protein molecules.

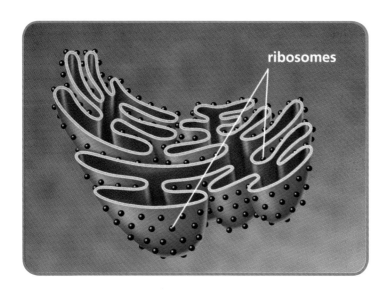

ribosomes

Some of the protein products made by ribosomes in the cytoplasm are ready to go. Others attach themselves to the surface of the **endoplasmic reticulum**, or ER. The ER is a network of tubes extending from the membrane of the nucleus. In the ER, an unfinished protein product continues its development. While in the ER, a short section of the insulin molecule is cut off and the remaining molecule is folded. The ER then transports the insulin to the **Golgi apparatus**.

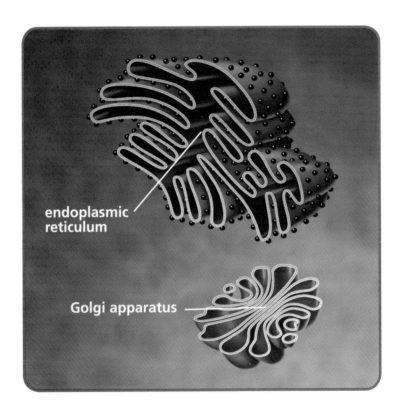

endoplasmic reticulum

Golgi apparatus

The Finishing Station

New molecules may need some finishing work. This is done in the Golgi apparatus, an organelle that looks like a stack of curved disks. In the case of insulin, a large section of amino acids is removed from the middle so the insulin can be used by the body.

The Golgi apparatus is also a packaging and delivery service. It packages fats, carbohydrates, and proteins in small bubbles called **vesicles**. Then it ships the materials to other locations in and out of the cell.

When an insulin molecule is finished, it is packaged in a vesicle along with many other insulin molecules. The vesicle fuses with the cell membrane, and the insulin is released from the cell. From here, it enters the bloodstream.

Scientist of Significance

The Golgi apparatus was named after Italian doctor Camillo Golgi. Golgi spent much of his medical career researching the nervous system. He developed a method of staining nervous system **tissue** samples so the paths of nerve cells could be seen for the first time. This method is still used today. It's called Golgi's method or Golgi staining.

Golgi used his staining technique to identify several types of cells and cell structures. In 1898, he discovered the organelle now known as the Golgi apparatus. In 1906, Golgi and another doctor, Santiago Ramón y Cajal, won the Nobel Prize for their discoveries about the nervous system.

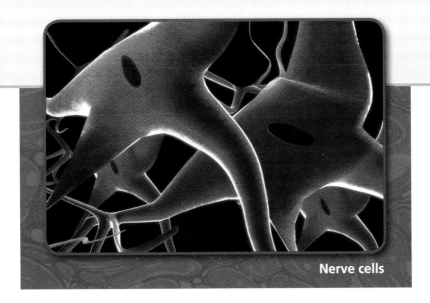

Nerve cells

The Janitorial Staff

Vacuoles are the storage organelles in a cell. Vacuoles are pockets or holes inside a cell that store water and nutrients until the cell needs them. Some vacuoles store waste until the cell is ready to get rid of it.

All cell processes produce some kind of waste. The waste may be leftover materials, broken cell parts, or harmful chemicals. To clean up the waste, cells have clean-up specialists called **lysosomes**. Lysosomes are small bubbles filled with digestive **enzymes**. Enzymes are proteins that cause reactions in cells. Each enzyme in the body is designed to do a specific job. Some of the enzymes in lysosomes digest nutrients for the cell. Others break down waste products.

Suicide Sacs

Lysosomes are sometimes called *suicide sacs*. When many lysosomes break, the enzymes within them dissolve everything inside, killing the cell. This process is one way a body can quickly break down unwanted or worn-out cells.

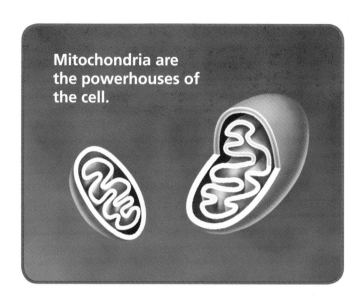

Mitochondria are the powerhouses of the cell.

The Power Source

A factory needs a source of energy, such as electricity, to power all of the equipment. To power cell processes such as protein assembly, cells need energy too. They get this energy from organelles called **mitochondria**. Mitochondria are like little power plants in a cell. They use oxygen to convert the energy stored in food to **ATP** (adenosine triphosphate). ATP is the form of energy that cells use to perform their jobs.

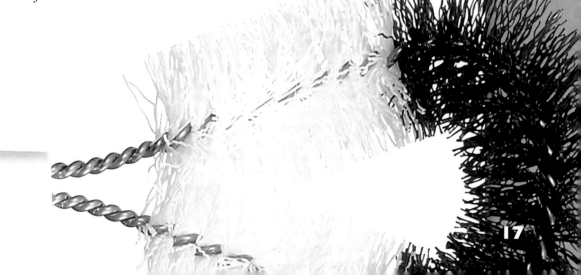

chapter three

From Food to
Energy

How does the food you eat become the ATP that cells need? Through metabolism. Metabolism is the series of chemical reactions in the cells of an organism that provides the energy and nutrients needed to live and grow. Metabolism in the human body includes **cellular respiration**. Cellular respiration is the process by which cells change molecules in food into a form of energy that cells can use.

Breaking Down What You Chow Down

There's energy stored in the sugars, starches, fats, and proteins that you eat. But your cells can't use this energy directly. It takes many enzymes and many steps to release this energy in the form of ATP, which your cells can use.

When you eat foods, digestive enzymes in the mouth, stomach, and small intestine break down large food molecules into their smaller building blocks. Starches are broken down into sugars. Proteins are broken down into amino acids. Fats are broken down into fatty acids. The smaller molecules are passed into the bloodstream and carried to cells throughout the body. When these simple molecules reach cells, they can be broken down for energy or used as building blocks to build more complex molecules.

Molecular model of adenosine triphosphate (ATP)

Inquire and Investigate: Enzymes

Question: Does the digestive enzyme amylase (AM uh lays) break down proteins?

Answer the question: I think that amylase _____.

Form a hypothesis: Amylase (does/does not) break down proteins.

Test the hypothesis:

Materials
- small box of gelatin mix
- shallow pan for the gelatin
- large plate
- teaspoon
- water
- three small bowls or glasses
- saliva (contains amylase)
- chunk of fresh pineapple (contains bromelain, a protein-digesting enzyme)
- three cotton balls

Procedure
- Follow the directions on the gelatin box. Place the pan of gelatin in the refrigerator until it's set.

- Cut three 4-inch squares of gelatin, and place them on the plate.

- Put a teaspoon of water in one bowl and a teaspoon of saliva in another. Squeeze the juice out of the pineapple chunk into the third bowl.

- Dip one cotton ball into the bowl of water, and place the ball on a gelatin square. (Water does not contain digestive enzymes. It is the control to compare the other reactions to.) Dip a second cotton ball into the pineapple juice, and place it on another square. Dip the third cotton ball into the saliva, and place it on the last square.

- Let the gelatin squares sit at room temperature for two hours and observe what happens.

Observations: The gelatin with the water cotton ball did not change. The gelatin with the pineapple juice began to liquefy. The gelatin with the saliva (amylase) did not change.

Conclusions: Amylase does not break down proteins. The enzyme in the pineapple juice did break down the proteins in the gelatin, which is what caused the gelatin to liquefy. Amylase, on the other hand, is an enzyme that breaks down starches, not proteins, so it had no effect on the gelatin. This supports the idea that each enzyme in the body has its own job.

Sugar Really Does Give You Energy!

Has your mom ever told you not to eat a lot of sugar because it will give you too much energy? Technically, she's correct. The breakdown of sugar does provide energy for your body. Sugar that enters a cell is broken down through the process of **glycolysis**. During glycolysis, a sugar molecule called *glucose* is split in half and two molecules of ATP are produced.

Greek Glycolysis

The word *glycolysis* comes from the Greek words *glyco* (sugar/sweet) and *lyse* (to break down or dissolve). So *glycolysis* literally means "to break down sugar."

There's still a lot of energy stored in the two halves of the sugar molecule. Now it's up to the mitochondria to break them down further and make even more ATP. So the two halves of the sugar molecule attach themselves to special transport molecules that move them into the mitochondria. There, a process called the **Krebs cycle** converts the molecule into two ATP molecules and several high-energy **electrons**.

The electrons are then transported to the electron transport chain in the membranes of the mitochondria. The electrons are passed from one molecule of the chain to the next, undergoing a series of chemical reactions. Each reaction gives off energy. This energy is used to build more ATP. At the end of the chain, oxygen atoms pick up the electrons along with charged hydrogen atoms and form water for the body.

In humans, cellular respiration results in 36 molecules of ATP. This energy gives cells the power they need to live, grow, and work.

chapter four

The Cell Cycle

Like all living things, cells reproduce, grow, and eventually die. Cells are "born" when one cell divides into two cells. This is called *cell division*. New cells then spend time growing and carrying out their jobs in the body until it's their turn to divide.

As a body grows, it requires more cells. When cells become worn-out or damaged, they need new cells to take their place. When new cells are needed by a body, existing cells reproduce, creating more cells.

You Can't Always Just Get New Ones!

Most cells in the body die on a regular basis and are replaced by new cells. Skin cells, for example, live only about 20 days before dying and being replaced by new skin cells. Other cells, such as brain and nerve cells, are meant to last a lifetime. These cells are not replaced when they die.

The Cell Cycle

The cycle of division and growth in cells is called the *cell cycle*. The cell cycle is divided into four phases—Gap 1, synthesis, Gap 2, and cell division.

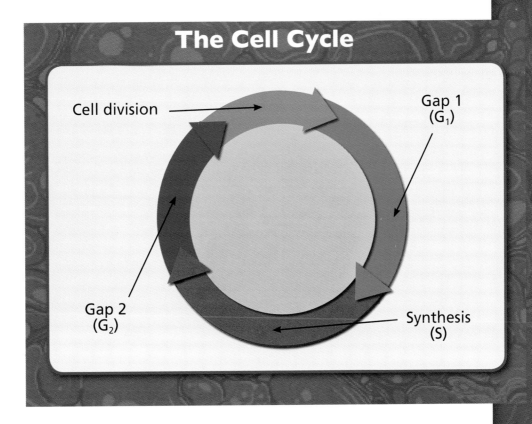

The Gap 1 phase (G_1) is the first and longest phase of the cycle. During the Gap 1 phase, a cell grows and carries out its normal life processes. It takes in nutrients, uses energy, makes proteins, and carries out many other functions.

At some point, a cell may receive a chemical signal that tells it to divide. The cell then enters the synthesis phase (S). During this phase, the cell makes a copy of every strand, or **chromosome**, of DNA in its nucleus. A human body cell has 23 pairs of chromosomes to copy.

The cell then enters the Gap 2 phase (G_2). It continues to grow and produce proteins that are needed for division. When it's ready, it moves into the cell division phase.

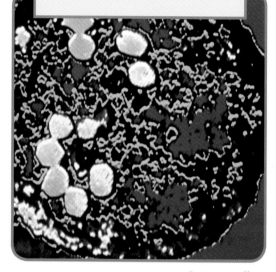

Cancer cells

A Permanent Phase

Some types of cells, such as muscle and nerve cells, don't divide once they mature. Instead of moving to the synthesis phase, these cells enter a resting phase called G_0 and stay there for the rest of their lives.

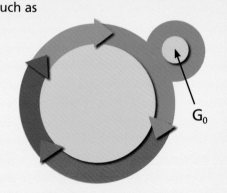

G_0

Mitosis is the first stage in cell division. During mitosis, the DNA that was duplicated in the synthesis phase is carefully sorted so that each daughter cell gets the exact same DNA that the parent cell had before the DNA was copied. This happens in a series of steps. First the membrane around the cell's nucleus breaks down. When the original and copied chromosomes are no longer contained, they line up in the center of the cell. Then one of each type of chromosome moves toward opposite ends of the cell. When each side of the cell has a complete set of chromosomes, the cell is ready to divide into two separate cells.

All in the Family

When cells reproduce, the original cell is called the *parent cell* and the new cells are called *daughter cells*.

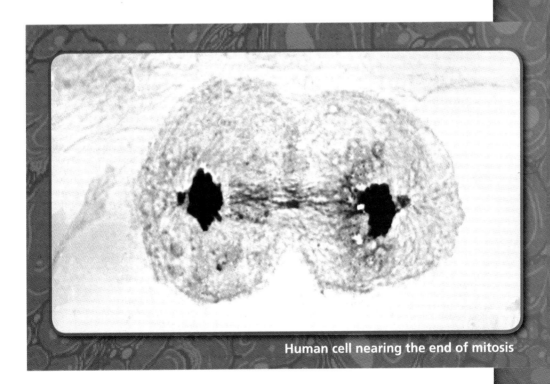

Human cell nearing the end of mitosis

The second stage of cell division is **cytokinesis**. Cytokinesis is the process of pinching the cell in half. As the cell begins to constrict around the middle, a new membrane forms around each set of chromosomes. This creates a new nucleus with a complete set of identical chromosomes for each new cell. By the time the cell pinches completely in half, the two new cells are ready for life on their own.

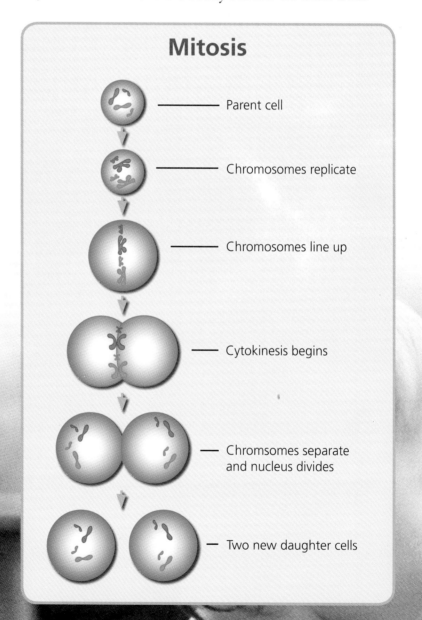

Mitosis

Parent cell

Chromosomes replicate

Chromosomes line up

Cytokinesis begins

Chromsomes separate and nucleus divides

Two new daughter cells

Meiosis

Not all cells in the human body divide through mitosis. The cells used for sexual reproduction (to create babies) form through a process called **meiosis**. These cells are known as **gametes**. When cells divide through meiosis, each gamete ends up with only half of the chromosomes present in the original parent cell. When a male and female gamete join, they combine chromosomes, forming offspring with a complete set of chromosomes for their cells. Since each half of the chromosomes came from a different set of DNA, the new cells are not identical to either parent cell as they are in mitosis. This is why all human beings, other than identical siblings, have unique DNA.

Tracing the Path of Science

Chromosome discovery began in the mid-1800s when these strands of DNA were first observed in plant cells. Then in 1879, German scientist Walther Flemming noticed small "threads" in the center of dividing animal cells. Because these threads absorbed the colored stains he was using to view the cells, Flemming called them the "stainable substance of the nucleus" or "chromatins." As he studied the threads, Flemming noticed that they moved in orderly patterns from the start of cell division to the finish. Flemming drew and described these patterns and gave the process of cell division a name—*mitosis*, which came from the Greek word for "thread."

In 1888, another scientist, Heinrich Waldeyer, was studying these important "threads." He called them *chromosomes* (Greek for "colored bodies"), and the name stuck.

Through his experiments with fruit flies in the early 1900s, Thomas Hunt Morgan showed that genes are found on chromosomes. A few years later, the first "mapping" of a chromosome was completed.

Finally, in the 1940s, Oswald Avery's experiments with bacteria demonstrated that chromosomes contain the DNA that determines hereditary traits (characteristics passed on from generation to generation). This became the basis for modern DNA research.

chapter five

Cellular
Current Events

While much has been learned about cells and how they work, there is still a lot to learn. Research on cells is ongoing, and each new discovery brings changes to the medical field.

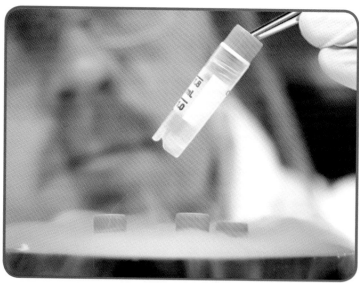

Cells being cryopreserved (frozen) for DNA research

Artificial Vesicles

Vesicles play a very important role in the transport and delivery of materials around the body. Artificial vesicles called *liposomes* have been created to learn more about how real vesicles function. They are also used to deliver materials to cells in the body.

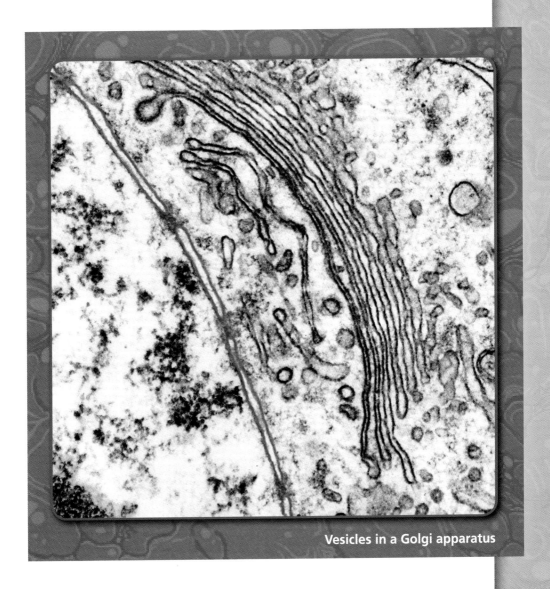

Vesicles in a Golgi apparatus

Vesicles deliver proteins where they're needed. But how does a vesicle know where to go and when to release its contents? In 1993, biologist James Rothman discovered several proteins in cell and vesicle membranes that he called SNARE proteins. These SNARE proteins seemed to bind in ways that control where a vesicle will fuse with a membrane. Rothman was able to re-create these proteins and build his own artificial vesicles. He used these liposomes to provide insights into how proteins guide vesicle transport and delivery.

Currently, some cancer-fighting drugs are packaged into liposomes to be delivered to cancerous cells in patients' bodies. The vesicles are engineered to bind only to cancer cells, so the drugs contained in them don't invade healthy cells. This allows doctors to fight cancers with much smaller doses of drugs, causing far fewer side effects.

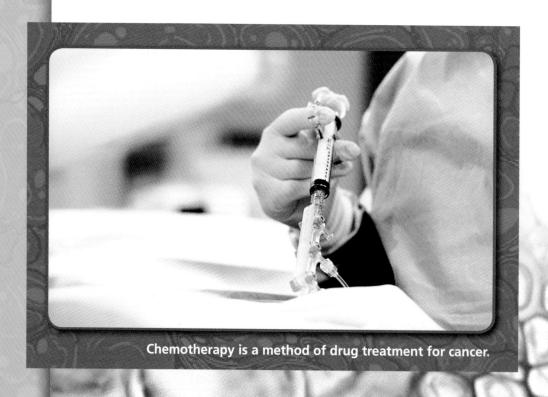

Chemotherapy is a method of drug treatment for cancer.

Unfortunately, clever cancer cells have found a way to fight back. Scientists have found that some cancer cells can repackage cancer-fighting drugs into new vesicles and then "spit them out." Scientists continue to study how cancer cells do this, hoping they may be able to find ways to prevent it.

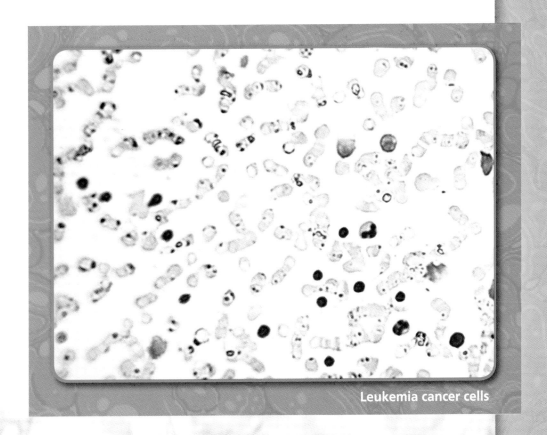

Leukemia cancer cells

The Mitochondria of Youth

Scientists have known for a while that energy-converting mitochondria have their own DNA. More recently, however, scientists working with mice discovered that mutations in mitochondria DNA may affect aging. A mutation is a change in a gene or chromosome. Most mutations have no effect on cells. A few can be harmful. In the studies, mice with more mutations in their mitochondria aged faster than other mice. It is believed that the mutations prevented the cells from doing normal maintenance, thereby increasing the aging process.

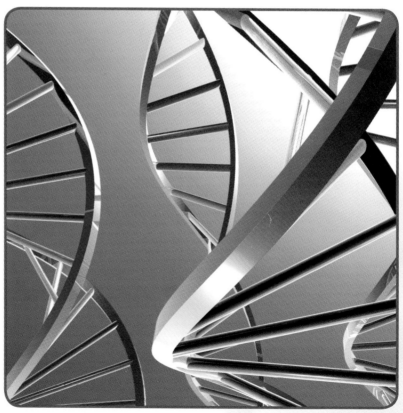

DNA helix

Scientists are now working to develop and test enzymes that might be used to prevent mutations or repair damaged cells. Hopefully this research will someday help scientists slow the aging process in humans.

Warning! Stress Can Cause Cell Aging

Telomeres are areas at the ends of chromosomes that prevent chromosomes from unwinding during cell division. Telomeres slowly diminish each time a cell divides. The loss or shortening of telomeres has been linked to the aging process because once a telomere becomes too short, the cell stops dividing, ages, and dies.

Studies done by Dr. Elissa Epel and her colleagues at the University of California, San Francisco, have found that stress can speed up the shortening of telomeres. Too much stress can affect the production of an enzyme that usually helps replenish telomeres. Without enough of this enzyme, telomeres break down faster than normal. Epel's studies show this to be especially true in women. Researchers hope that future studies will determine other factors involved in the shortening of telomeres and whether men's cells are equally affected by stress.

Stem Cell Controversy

When an egg cell is **fertilized**, it begins dividing. After many divisions, it becomes a ball of cells. All of these cells are the same. None of them has started to turn into nerve cells, muscle cells, or other kinds of cells. These identical cells are known as stem cells.

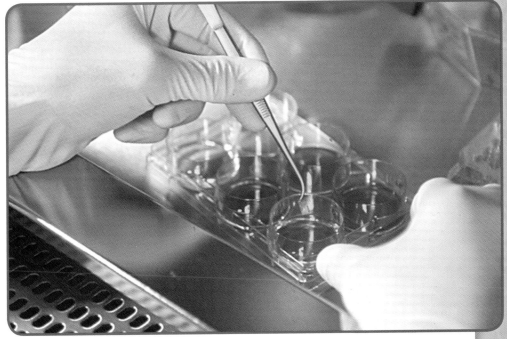

Stem cell research

As an embryo begins to grow, most of the stem cells start to differentiate, or become different types of cells. But even after birth, some stem cells remain in the human body. For example, stem cells in bone marrow can later divide to produce specialized blood cells when needed.

An Explanation of *Embryo*

When a fertilized egg cell begins to grow inside its mother, it is called an *embryo*. It is considered an embryo up to eight weeks of age, at which time it is called a *fetus* until birth.

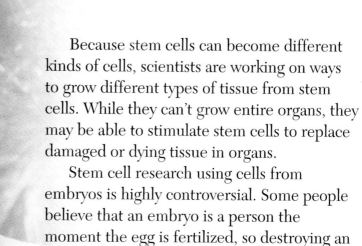

Because stem cells can become different kinds of cells, scientists are working on ways to grow different types of tissue from stem cells. While they can't grow entire organs, they may be able to stimulate stem cells to replace damaged or dying tissue in organs.

Stem cell research using cells from embryos is highly controversial. Some people believe that an embryo is a person the moment the egg is fertilized, so destroying an embryo to get stem cells is the same as killing a person. Others believe that an embryo with undifferentiated cells cannot feel or sense and, therefore, is not a person yet. Scientists have to weigh the moral dilemma of stem cell research with the possible benefits of successful stem cell use.

There are also less controversial types of stem cell research. Currently, stem cells taken from adults can develop into a few types of tissues. These tissues carry the donor's genes and can be used to replace damaged tissues in the donor with little danger of rejection. It is hoped that someday cells taken from adults will be able to be used to cure many types of diseases.

* * *

Scientists continue to study the mysteries of the human cell. They are investigating cell division, aging, and death, hoping to use the information to help people live longer, healthier lives. Cell research is far from complete, and the discoveries made today may affect everyone's health in the future.

Internet Connections and Related Reading for Cell Processes

http://www.cellsalive.com
Get the basics of cell biology, and then interact with cellular models, the cell cycle, and cell division.

http://www.biology4kids.com/files/cell_main.html and
http://www.biology4kids.com/files/cell2_main.html
Biology4Kids introduces you to the structure and function of cells in the human body.

http://library.thinkquest.org/C004535/introduction.html
This "Cellupedia" of knowledge includes information on cell basics, anatomy, and processes.

http://www.bbc.co.uk/schools/gcsebitesize/biology/cellprocesses/
1cellfunctionsrev1.shtml and http://www.bbc.co.uk/schools/
gcsebitesize/biology/cellprocesses/celldivisionrev1.shtml
Grab some "bite-size" knowledge about cells and cell functions. Then follow up by "snacking" on some facts about cell division.

http://nobelprize.org/medicine/educational/2001/
Become the Cell Division Supervisor in the "Control of the Cell Cycle" game to review how the cell cycle works.

* * *

Human Body by the DK Publishing Staff. This Eyewitness Science book on the human body includes information on cells. Dorling Kindersley, 2004. ISBN 0-7566-0688-8. [RL 7.9 IL 5–9] (2395706 HB)

The Human Body by Nicholas Harris. Zoom in for a closer look at the human body, including its organs and systems. The Gale Group, 2002. ISBN 1-5671-1693-0. [RL 4 IL 4–7] (6870606 HB)

•RL = Reading Level
•IL = Interest Level

Perfection Learning's catalog numbers are included for your ordering convenience. HB indicates hardback.

Glossary

amino acid   (uh MEEN oh AS id) molecule that makes up proteins

ATP   (ay tee pee) molecule that cells use directly for energy; adenosine triphosphate

cell membrane   (sel MEM brayn) thin, flexible band around a cell that controls the movement of substances in and out of the cell

cellular respiration   (SEL you ler res per AY shuhn) process of changing food molecules into ATP

chromosome   (KROH muh zohm) structural unit inside a cell's nucleus that carries genes made up of DNA

cytokinesis   (seye toh kuh NEE sis) division of the cytoplasm during mitosis or meiosis

DNA   (dee en ay) molecule that contains genetic information for making proteins; deoxyribonucleic acid

electron   (ee LEK trahn) tiny, negatively charged particle in an atom

endoplasmic reticulum   (en doh PLAZ mik ruh TIK you luhm) network of long tubes that extend from a cell's nucleus into its cytoplasm to form, store, and transport materials within the cell

enzyme   (EN zeyem) protein that causes chemical reactions inside a cell

fertilize   (FER tuh leyez) to unite a male and female cell (gametes) to produce a baby

gamete   (GAM eet) cell used for sexual reproduction

gene   (jeen) segment of DNA that contains information for making a particular protein

glycolysis (gleye KAHL uh sis) process of breaking down glucose, or sugar, molecules

Golgi apparatus (GAWL jee ap uh RAT uhs) organelle that modifies, stores, packages, and delivers materials in a cell

Krebs cycle (krebs SEYE kuhl) series of reactions in mitochondria that converts sugars into ATP; one of the steps in cellular respiration

lysosome (LEYE suh sohm) organelle that breaks down materials in a cell

meiosis (meye OH sis) process of dividing the nucleus of a cell that results in gamete formation

mitochondria (meye tuh KAHN dree uh) organelles that use oxygen to provide a cell with energy

mitosis (meye TOH sis) process of dividing the nucleus of a cell that results in two identical cells

nucleus (NOO klee uhs) organelle that controls a cell's activities

protein (PROH teen) large molecule made up of amino acids that helps with the growth, repair, and replacement of cells

ribosome (REYE buh sohm) organelle that makes proteins

tissue (TISH you) group of similar cells working together

vacuole (VAK yuh wohl) organelle that stores materials in a cell

vesicle (VES uh kuhl) small sac that stores or transports materials in a cell

Index

amino acids, 11, 19

ATP (adenosine triphosphate), 17, 19, 21

Avery, Oswald, 27

Brown, Robert, 6

cell cycle, 22–27

cell differentiation, 9, 35–36

cell history, 5–6

cell membranes, 11

cell shape, 8

cell size, 8

cell theory, 6

cells and the aging process, 32–33, 34

cellular respiration, 18–21

chromosomes, 24, 25, 26, 27, 32, 34

cytoplasm, 13

DNA (deoxyribonucleic acid), 12–13, 24, 25, 27, 32

electron transport, 21

endoplasmic reticulum, 11, 14

enzymes, 16, 19, 20, 33

Epel, Elissa, 34

eukaryotic cells, 12

Flemming, Walther, 27

genes, 12–13

glycolysis, 21

Golgi apparatus, 11, 14–15

Golgi, Camillo, 15

Hooke, Robert, 5

Krebs cycle, 21

lysosomes, 11, 16

meiosis, 27

metabolism, 18

microscopes, 5, 6, 7

mitochondria, 11, 17, 32–33

mitosis, 25–26, 27

Morgan, Thomas Hunt, 27

mRNA, 13

nucleus, 6, 11, 12

organelles, 10

prokaryotic cells, 12

proteins, 11

ribosomes, 11, 13

Rothman, James, 30

Ruska, Ernst, 7

Schleiden, Matthias, 6

Schwann, Theodor, 6

stem cells, 35–36

telomeres, 34

tRNA, 13

vacuoles, 16

van Leeuwenhoek, Anton, 5

vesicles, 15, 29–31
    liposomes, 29–31

Virchow, Rudolph, 6

Waldeyer, Heinrich, 27